MASSACRE IN NEWTOWN
Adam Lanza's Dark Passage to Madness

Other books by the author:

A PASSION FOR INNOCENCE - Sex and Sexuality
in the Paintings of John Currin

THE REFUGE OF SURFACES - A Poetics of Surfaces
and the Postmodern Odyssey

LET THERE BE LINKS - The Sources and Nature
of Internet Religion

Henry Berry has a long and broad background in philosophy,
literature, and art. With degrees in philosophy from Fairfield
University and Georgetown University, for over twenty years he
has worked in the fields of writing, publishing, and teaching.
Editor and ghostwriter for books on history and social critique,
creative writing teacher, reviewer of books on art and cultural
studies, editor/publisher of "The Small Press Book Review,"
author of articles and a publishing trade-newsletter column, and
publishing consultant are among the activities he has engaged in
over this time. He can be reached at **henryberryinct@gmail.com**.

MASSACRE IN NEWTOWN

Adam Lanza's Dark Passage to Madness

by Henry Berry

Henry Berry
PO Box 176
Southport, CT 06890

henryberryinct@gmail.com

CONTENT

Introduction

On December 14, 2112, a Friday, a few minutes after 9:30AM, Adam Lanza armed with a semiautomatic Bushmaster rifle and two handguns forced his way into the Sandy Hook Elementary School in Newtown, Connecticut. He got into the school by shooting out the plate glass of one of the front doors which had been locked as a security measure. Killing the school principle and guidance counselor who confronted him upon rushing from a meeting room as he made his way down a hallway, after a quick detour to look into the main office and fire a couple of shots into a closed door behind which other adults were hiding, Lanza continued down the hallway to two first-grade classrooms where he cornered and shot to death twenty children aged six and seven and their teachers. Before leaving the house where he lived with his mother Nancy Lanza, Adam Lanza shot her to death in her bedroom. By the time the rampage was over, twenty-seven people had been killed including the shooter. Adam Lanza shot himself in the head with one of the handguns he had brought into the school with him to the sound of sirens blaring as town police and other first responders raced to the scene.

This is a sketchy picture of the awful event from murder of the mother to suicide of the shooter. In the following pages, many more details will be attached to facts recounted in this sketch. From such clusters of facts, associations and links between and among them, and consideration of facts, incidents, and circumstances surrounding the core of the incident as sketched above, readings of these, analyses, interpretations, inferences, and hypotheses will be proffered.

Lieutenant Paul Vance, a Connecticut state trooper who is the official spokesperson regarding the incident appearing regularly in televised news conferences in the days following the massacre, says that the investigation will take some time, possibly many months or over a year. Although the perpetrator is dead, the general course and facts of the incident are indisputably known, and there will be no trial, the investigation is regarded as and being conducted as a criminal investigation so the required resources can be utilized to try to search for answers to questions arising in any crime which may provide some consolation to relatives of the victims and help to prevent future mass murders of this kind. Even though the official investigation will probably be going on after this study of mine is published and possibly long beyond publication, whatever evidence turns up, conclusions made, and hypotheses proposed, these will not contradict or negate the perspectives, analyses, and interpretations of this study. For such perspectives, analyses, and interpretations of mine will be tied to indisputable physical evidence, interconnections, and actions. For example, while little is known about the nature and quality of the relationship between the mother Nancy Lanza and the son Adam Lanza and as I suppose, little will ever be known considering that this relationship occurred mostly within their Newtown house, what is known is that Adam Lanza's first victim was his mother; and she was killed in her bedroom with multiple gun shots to her face.

Any points I make or analyses I engage in with respect to the mother-son relationship which is an essential topic of such a study (as well as the crime investigation) will be directly and clearly tied to the fact of the relationship and of the murder of the mother as well as its place in the sequence of documented, indisputable events. Thus insights, perspectives, analyses, interpretations, and inferences of mine, while some may take them as premature, could only be supplemented by later ones coming from official investigators and others; or mine would be seen as preliminary considerations or as supplementing later studies based on additional findings--which ever way you want to look at it. The point is that in sticking to indisputable data to proffer the meaning of it, this study can not being going down the wrong track in relation to later reports or studies to follow.

Although this study "Massacre in Newtown" is made up largely of organization of documented, indisputable evidence, relationships, circumstances, and actions, such a study inevitably calls for some "mind-reading" and personality analysis of the deranged perpetrator. Since the mind and personality of anyone can never be fully known or comprehended, my thoughts on this aspect of the murderous event in Newtown may be different from and debated by others including criminal investigators, psychologists called on by these or the media for their views, and writers in the area of true-crime and psychological elements of contemporary culture.

My interests, activities, and background going into this study are undergraduate and graduate (M.A.) degrees in philosophy, decades of literary and art criticism as a book reviewer, and lifelong student of psychology, contemporary (postmodern) culture, and media. Freud and Nietzsche are two thinkers I have studied extensively and deeply. In the days of my interest in fiction, Nabokov was the writer I was most interested in, reading not only many of his novels and stories, but also biographies of him.

1. Locale and Motive

The question of motive is inevitably, compellingly the most
burning question in serious crimes, particularly mass murders.
With regard to the Newtown massacre, it has been announced
through the official spokesman Lt. Paul Vance that the focus of the
criminal investigation will be to answer the question of motive, the
question of "why?" the massacre happened. Why did Adam Lanza
heavily arm himself and set off on a killing spree ending in the
deaths of twenty elementary-school children and seven adults?
Vance and others who have been interviewed such as FBI agents,
psychologists, and mental-health counselors usually couple
mention that motive is a key question with the proviso that this
may never be know because Adam Lanza committed suicide, and
no suicide notes or other writings have been found and he went so
far as to destroy the hard drives on computers found in his
Newtown home where he lived with his mother.

Considering that the motive may never be known or may at best be
guesswork on the basis of education, experience, and professional
training and work, study of the physical locale where the shootings
took place takes on a larger part in trying to solve the "puzzle" (to
use Vance's word) of the crime. The locale can become a bigger
piece of the puzzle than it ordinarily is in trying to answer the
question of motive in most crimes of serious and deadly injury to
others. While motive as strictly understood as rooted in an
individual's mental state, and the effects of experiences, elements

of the moment, and such cannot be determined from a study of the locale, an explanation for why it was that the many children were shot emerges.

Considering the absence of any evidence or observations ordinarily going to shed light on motive and the probable ambiguity of any evidence or observations which would become known, what study of the locale seems to indicate about the pattern of behavior and the line of its course will probably come the closest to getting at motive which will come about from investigation. Study of the locale with tracing the known, indisputable track and actions of Adam Lanza yields a continuum and series of impulses from which one can deduce mental states and processes making up the heated, blinkered, emotion-infused mindset--perhaps better called skewered excited awareness or ineluctable sense of urgency-- bringing on the event and accounting for its stages. Since Adam Lanza's mind to which one would look for motives cannot be examined by talk with him nor by writings, habits, or other activities or relationships which are regarded as the next best material for understanding another's mind after scrutiny allowed by direct talk with an individual, study of behavior and actions within the context of the locale in which the event began and ended is probably the best one can do in trying to surmise what there is about an individual's mind taken as accounting for motive. Since mental states and processes shape actions, initial actions (which are initiating actions), the sequence of actions (including time), and specifics of actions can be studied for some grasp and some sense of mental states and processes. And the study of actions within the context of a locale can add to this sense and grasp.

What I mean by "locale" in this study to begin to try to comprehend the massacre includes not only the geography of the area, but also development within it with particular attention to buildings where large numbers of persons would be gathered.

2. Newtown, Connecticut

Newtown is about 60 square miles in size, Connecticut's fifth largest town in area. It is tucked into an area of northeast Fairfield County bordering adjacent New Haven county. Though large in area, Newtown can be described as "tucked in" because it has a removed, almost timeless, certainly quiet ambience. The superhighway route 25 cutting north off of Route 15, the Merritt Parkway turning into the Wilbur Cross Parkway past Stratford, ends as a superhighway well south of Newtown in Trumbull. There it continues north through Trumbull and Monroe until reaching Newtown and going beyond through Danbury and other parts north mostly as a well-traveled two-lane (one each way) primary roadway in a moderately-populated, moderately-developed area. Much of Route 25 is commercially developed with single buildings for larger businesses such as supermarkets and with rows of attached spaces for smaller businesses such as restaurants, consignment shops, newsstands, medical offices, and other types of services and goods sought by the surrounding suburban, relatively affluent population.

This commercial development of Route 25 continues into the northern part of where the roadway goes through Newtown. Shortly after this, a little past where you can take a right on Mile

Hill Road becoming quickly Wasserman Way Road to get to connections to the east-west superhighway Route 84, the commercial development ends. Going along Route 25, you approach Newtown center with part of a golf course to your left and past it on the same side a park. At the juncture with Route 302 coming in from the left where there is a light, you see the small police station at little up on the left. Going farther up Route 25, you pass through what is considered the heart and also the pride of Newtown, the Newtown Borough Historic District. Along this part for about a mile are large older homes left and right interspersed at points with a few businesses such as a restaurant which are converted houses and public buildings including the Cyrenius H. Booth Library and the Edmond Town Hall. The one anomaly along this central road of the District is the General Daniel Baldwin House standing out for its Georgian style. The few small businesses in this stretch through the center of Newtown are like businesses in a small village, small in size and small in purpose-- the branch of a bank, country lawyers' offices, a general store, a printing shop.

The center of the center of the Newtown Borough Historic District, the civic omphalos of many an American small town, is a tall flagpole almost always flying a large American flag. At this flagpole, you can take a right onto Route 6 heading east, known to residents as Church Hill Road. The farther you go from the Borough along Route 25, the more dense become the commercial establishments along this road which is another one of Newtown's main roads. About a mile along it are other connectors to Route 84 taking drivers into or out of Newtown. By these connectors is a large diner and a gas station. Here one could be at almost any major highway on and off ramps anywhere in America.

Route 6 which is also Route 84 for a stretch ends here. The roadway keeps the name Church Hill Road. But once you cross the bridge over Route 84 and it is behind you, you are on Route 34. A little way along it, you again start running into small businesses along the roadside letting you know that you have not left Newtown. These businesses are older and are rougher, more functional, buildings than the buildings along Route 25 which are newer in a part of the town which was developed later. This older, simpler, more rustic part of Newtown is known as Sandy Hook.

After a group of small businesses making a small business center for nearby residents, Route 34 turns sharply right. This was the direction Adam Lanza came from his home on Yogananda Street about five miles away. Lanza took a right off Route 34 (also called Berkshire Road along this portion of it). You leave Route 34 by going straight, putting yourself on Riverside Road. Taking this a couple of miles farther by plain houses on country plots requiring little landscaping whose small numbers dwindle more as the wooded terrain grows thicker, eventually you get to the dead end of Riverside Road at the Housatonic River which is the border between Newtown and Southbury. Thinly populated and ending in a dead end, Riverside Road doesn't get much traffic; although this picks up some during the height of the summer when boaters, picnickers, and hikers make their way to the Housatonic River for recreation.

Most of the traffic there is on Riverside Road turns right at Dickenson Road less than half a mile in. By the entrance of Dickenson is a volunteer firehouse. At the end of Dickenson Road is the Sandy Hook Elementary School.

Large in area as Newtown is, the interstate Route 84 takes you through the town in about five minutes. From the interstate to drivers whisking through at sixty or seventy or more miles per hour, there is nothing distinctive or exceptional about Newtown. The rolling, wooded land stretching out on either side of 84 looks like any other rolling, stretching land along parts of the interstates running through inland Connecticut. Since the interstate completed decades ago, Newtown's major roadways Routes 25, 302, and 6 are now used primarily by Newtown residents to get to different parts of town. Apart from the commercially-developed parts of Route 25 and the group of small businesses on Route 34 in Sandy Hook and another on Route 302, the rest of Newtown's large area is residential. The yards of the houses along Route 25 in the Borough and on nearby streets are not generally large, though some are. Once you are away from this historical civic center, the yards become larger and the houses bigger. There are neighborhoods of modern colonials, split levels, ranch houses, and other modern types built by developers; but these are limited and found mostly near the borders of adjacent towns which have mostly this kind of housing so they do not figure much into characterizing Newtown or its image.

The farther you get from the Newtown Borough with its Historic District and onto the back roads, what are seen as the yards of houses change into what is better called a house and surrounding grounds. On many of these, the grounds sprawl so extensively rising and dipping that there are spots from which you could not even see the respective house. Along with the Historic District, these country homes and estates go into characterizing Newtown. Along with its outstanding education, historic district, and small-town atmosphere, the feel of living--of actually being--in the country while still in affluent, bustling, populous Fairfield County is a primary appeal of Newtown.

In nearby towns such as Easton, Redding, and Brookfield, you can find older homes on large parcels of land with old trees, fields, stone and wooden fences, and brooks. But these towns do not have a center like Newtown's. Thus they do not have the focused, overt community spirit of Newtown. While such nearby towns have small shopping districts for daily necessities such as basic groceries and gas, they do not have the variety of small businesses and professional services such a legal and medical as Newtown. Other nearby towns such as Oxford and Southbury, though old, were officially incorporated as towns in the later 1700s; whereas Newtown was incorporated in 1711 making it one of the oldest towns in the region and accounting for the Colonial and Revolutionary War historical eras reflected in the town's attachment to and ongoing interest in history.

With Newtown's genuine and self-confident tie to early American history and its expanses of thinly-populated and unpopulated country of woods, fields, and undulating land, the town uniquely blends a particular civic spirit and comfortable, comforting way of life embodying and expressing idealized American values. In summarizing Newtown so radio listeners and TV viewers could quickly grasp the environment in which the massacre took place, many early media reports used terms such as "Norman Rockwell portrait" and "picture perfect." These apply.

3. The Choice of Schools

It's about five miles by road to Sandy Hook Elementary School from Yogananda Street where Adam Lanza lived with his mother Nancy. Most of this is along Route 34. Yogananda Street connects to Osborne Hill Road and Bresson Farm Road. Depending on which way you want to go, you take either of these to Bennetts Bridge Road, which leads you to Route 34. At Route 34, Adam Lanza took a right to get to the School.

Yogananda Street is in an hilly area in the northeastern part of Newtown. It is about as far out of the center of Newtown, Newtown Borough, that you can go and still be in Newtown. It is a more recently developed area of Newtown of large newer homes on large lots. Like parts of Newtown away from the center close to Newtown's borders with adjacent towns, with many of the roads in this area ending in dead ends by design or by the Housatonic River close by, the network of roads creates a natural neighborhood. The three or so such neighborhoods of the area are distinctly upscale. Swimming pools are frequent, landscaping is professional, driveways are paved, walkways lead to all the doorways, yards are kept up. Most of the residents are relative newcomers to Newtown, purchasing these newer homes constructing for them as Newtown grew inevitably not only from its attractions, but also its proximity to cities such as Bridgeport, Danbury, and Waterbury, and for some commuters, the cities of New Haven, Stamford, and Hartford further away where business executives and professionals such as lawyers hold well-paying jobs. The cleared, landscaped areas for the houses set back from the well-kept, newer roads are surrounded by woods. As you go along Bennetts Bridge Road toward Route 34, you pass by two large fields, as if a border between the neighborhood including Yogananda Street and the wider world.

Having taken a right out of Bennetts Bridge Road, Adam Lanza would have passed by other inviting prospective target locations between where he lived and the elementary school. The first of these about three miles down Route 34 was Newtown High School. With about 1800 students and 125 teachers, it might have been a good target. However, to get close to the school building set back from the road, you have to pull into an opening with two entrance lanes and two for exit separated by a strip of grass rimmed with stones. Near the far end of this strip is a small building little larger than a closet. It looks like it could be post for a security guard; but it was never manned, and its purpose is unclear. (This was before the shooting at the elementary school down the road.). Nonetheless, the small building and grass strip presented features where there could be someone perhaps repairing something or doing something on the strip of lawn. The closer Lanza could get to the target location without being closely seen by anyone, the better.

There were other circumstances making an assault on the high-school problematic and unappealing beyond these considerations to be faced right after Lanza would turn into the entrance. Once past the building and inside the complex, you can turn right into a smaller parking lot, veer left to the larger parking lot across from the front entrance, or go straight to the entrance. Whichever way you go, your approach to the school building is visible for a hundred or so yards. Moreover, you would have to park your car and walk a way to get to the building with the hope of entering unseen or remaining unseen driving straight to the front entrance. Once Lanza was out of his car carrying his weapons and dressed in military-style clothing with the utility vest loaded with ammunition, his plan was sprung. The instant he was seen, alarm would start to spread. Newtown High School was not conducive to the element of surprise required for killing the maximum number of targets possible.

Besides, Newtown High School is a huge building, cavernous. After renovations ending in January 2011, it is 376,000 square feet, about 300,000 square feet before the renovations. Adam Lanza would not have had to ever been in the high-school building since its renovations to know its immense size was daunting to one planning an assault intended to shoot to death as many individuals as possible in a short time. Then there were those in the building. Assuming Lanza somehow made it into the building unnoticed dressed in black and carrying a rifle, grown men who were teachers and older teens many of whom were athletic would not make the best targets. Though there were hundreds and hundreds of targets--close to 2,000--they would be spread over a wide area. With the conceived killing zone so expansive, chances for maximum deaths and casualties were reduced. Even a deranged mind could figure this; to a murderous deranged mind, this would be a salient factor in contemplating a desirable strategy.

In the high school, at the first sounds of shooting, older youngsters by now cognizant of defensive flight and adult teachers would flee away from the gunfire into far reaches of the building and probably out doorways found at all parts of it. With the building's labyrinthine hallways, different floors, locker rooms, laboratories, offices for the relatively large teaching and administrative staff, many lavatories, and with the renovations, a greenhouse, despite their large number, individuals were be scattering in all directions away from the gunfire or else huddled in groups in many rooms with unknown configurations frightened out of their wits or surely in some cases, preparing defensive measures. Many of the doors would probably quickly be barricaded. And should the heavily-armed intruder manage to find an easily accessible room or break through a barricade, older teens and adults, even many of the females, would be strong enough and aware enough to throw desks or other objects at him or to take their chances and rush him as a group to easily overpower him.

Hunting down teens and teachers would had fled but were still in the building would not only interrupt the shooter's deadly intent, but also leave him vulnerable even though heavily armed. Some of the male teachers would likely have the military background or presence of mind to be planning to bring an end to the deadly spree. All along the hundreds of yards to go in the cavernous, multi-storied building to find new victims, stopping here and there along the way to test closed doors, a hostile-minded intruder would be becoming more vulnerable by the minute from older persons devising varied defensive measures and also police and other responders who would certainly be racing toward the high school within minutes after the first rounds of gunfire broke out.

Other approaches to the high school were no more inviting. Oakview Road running behind the school as it faces Route 34 offers an alternative to the front entrance. This road runs the length of Newtown Hill School facing away from Route 34. Lanza could have parked somewhere along this road to approach the school. But doorways which would be back doorways would probably be locked; and they would probably not be glass doorways which could be easily shot out.

Baseball fields and other parking lots away from primary doorways at other approaches to the school presented even worse prospects for a surprise attack.

Newtown High School was not a propitious target for mass murder. Reed Middle School not far from the high school was a more inviting target. Turning left off Route 34 onto Wasserman Way just before the entranceway to the high school, the school was about half a mile down the road. Like the high school, Reed Middle School was in a largely rural and unwooded part of Newtown. One imagines large farms with crops and animals in this area in the seventeen and eighteen hundreds. With about 1,000 middle-grade students and their teachers and administrators, Reed offered a target-rich site. Nonetheless, like the high school, it presented problems for an assailant wanting to work more efficiently, most destructively.

Reed was accessible enough by turning right just before the buildings onto Trades Lane. As with the high school though, parking in the larger front lot or the smaller one behind the school left you having to walk a way to the school, possibly observed all the way. Or if you wanted to have the advantage of surprise, you could take a left off Trades Lane and instead of taking another quick left into the front parking lot, stay on the lane running along the front of the school to the front entrance. But once here, the advantage of surprise would most likely soon be lost. Leaving the car at the spot on the lane closest to the front entrance as one could get, one would then have to cross an open area like a small plaza of about twenty yards. Across this open area, one would come to a long row of glass doorways like doors leading into a movie theater. These opened onto a large atrium-like area that was usually nearly deserted. There wouldn't be many targets here; and some of the small number who might be would likely immediately start scattering in different directions spreading the alarm.

Once into the building, assuming he got this far, an assailant still wouldn't be near the heart of the school where targets would be gathered in groups--rows of classrooms. In the spacious atrium-like area, the assailant could turn left or right toward the gymnasium or the auditorium respectively. In either place, there would probably be students and teachers. But they would have much space in which to flee; and because of uncertainty about a good number of targets and the large space over which prospective targets would spread, neither the gymnasium or the auditorium were attractive for an assailant.

As Adam Lanza did in forgoing entering the cafeteria/auditorium to his right just inside the front entrance of the Sandy Hook Elementary School to proceed to his left to the classrooms, inside the front entrance at Reed Middle School, depending on which direction he turned, an assailant could pass by the gymnasium or auditorium to get to classrooms. But then it was a ways to classrooms along hallways past offices and secondary rooms with the advantage of surprise facing the possibility of slipping away with every second. And supposing a shooter did get to classrooms at Reed, here he would encounter circumstances similar to ones leading him to reject the high school as a favorable killing ground. Students would be older and not so helpless; more aware of the threat and likely to take better defensive measures including rushing to better avenues of flight available. There would be adult male teachers and administrators. Relatively sprawling and thus uncontrollable space, larger numbers of adults including males organizing resistance and escape, and older children introduced variables making Reed Middle School unattractive.

Besides such unacceptable variables attached directly to Reed, there were outside factors which might come into play to interfere with the planned carnage. Within five hundred yards of the school were at least five buildings where there could be individuals who would sound an alarm once the noisy mayhem broke out, with the possibility that one or more would make a rescue attempt, possibly being armed. The chance that no one would be at any of these buildings at the time of day of the planned assault was too great to consider. Moreover, the buildings would offer fleeing students and staff places to seek shelter and hide to thwart an assailant's plans should he have time to pursue these outside the school into the surrounding grounds.

And beyond the several buildings near Reed, there were others close by too with personnel certain to come to the aid of a school under assault and who would know how to act to bring an end to the threat. Within half a mile of Reed were the Garner Correctional Institution, a high-security state prison; the Newtown Municipal Center with offices for all types of town services and departments; and the headquarters of a company of the Governor's Horse Guard.

4. Confluence of Site and Madness

When you stop to think of it, by process of elimination, to a deranged individual bent on mass murder, Sandy Hook Elementary School stands out in the area as the best location for this sheerly on pragmatic grounds without getting into the thicket of psychosis and any possible malevolent will toward students and staff at this school.

As some mass murders have done, Adam Lanza could have gone to a shopping mall, movie theater, or other place where a sizable crowd of unsuspecting, vulnerable individuals would be sure to be. There are no malls or movie complexes in Newtown. To find these, you can go by Route 84 west to Danbury about 12 miles away; or to Waterbury about 18 miles away by 84 east. Going south on Route 25 onto the length where it becomes superhighway, you can find a huge mall about 15 miles away in Trumbull off of route 15, the Merritt Parkway. Or you could connect with Route 15 going east and past Stratford take a connector going south to Route 95 east to get to malls in Milford about 23 miles away. Big, major, shopping malls in Trumbull and Milford especially with diverse stores including national and regional chains, fast-food franchises, fashion boutiques, specialty shops, and esplanades with tables and chairs for resting and snacking draw large crowds of shoppers.

During the holiday shopping season in early December, these crowds would have been especially large at any time of any day. But to get to any of these kinds of locations for mass shootings increases the chances of getting stopped along the way and also of getting noticed before initiating the killing spree or before it could be underway for long. Parking lots as big as two or three or more football fields meant walking fifty or more yards garbed in combat-like gear and carrying a rifle--one major deterrent to selecting the high school or the middle school. Plus once inside where the shooting would begin, there would be all that space and all those stores for targets to run to--another deterrent. Driving to get to a large mall over such distances, there would also be the possibility of being noticed at a stop light by another driver or perhaps a pedestrian; or pulled over by a police car for a check about something or a minor traffic violation to thwart the plan even before it got started. All in all, Sandy Hook Elementary School is a clear preferable location.

Route 34 is a straight run to the school except for a little bit at either end from Yogananda Street to it and turning right off it onto Riverside Road for a short way until turning right again onto the short road Dickenson Road ending at the elementary school. It's less than three miles past Newtown High School on road where there is little traffic and no lights. About 9:15AM or so, well after considerable traffic of buses and cars relating to the start of the high school and middle school not far from each other for the day, there's not much traffic at all along Route 34. There are only two lights between where Lanza would get on Route 34 and Dickenson Road. If you aren't stopped by either one, you can get to the elementary school nonstop except for a couple of stop signs at intersections at either end of the Route 34 route, which would slow you down only a little. And even if you were stopped by a red light, there would not be a congestion of other drivers nor any pedestrians who might look curiously into your car.

There have been reports of an "altercation" between Adam Lanza and school personnel on the day before the shootings; which would be the Thursday. The cause of this has not been reported, if the mention is true and the cause is even known. But that Adam Lanza was at the school not long before the shootings and may have come into contact with school personnel is plausible; and it seems probable. As methodical as he was, he would have wanted to case the Sandy Hook Elementary School. Especially, he would have wanted to find out any notice people at the volunteer firehouse at the opening of Dickenson Road would take and how they might react. He'd also want to make sure he could get right to the school quickly once turning into Dickenson; that there was no construction, for example, nor a station for a security guard.

There's no way of knowing how many sites for the shooting Adam Lanza cased. As methodical and determined as he was, and as long a time as his disturbance was building to the stage of breaking out with mass murder, one supposes he would have thought about and investigated--cased--other sites besides Sandy Hook Elementary School. In just driving around Newtown on his own or with his mother in one of his infrequent errands outside the Yogananda Street home, Lanza would be taking in the overall layout, the roadways, the buildings, the traffic, the habits of pedestrians, the police presence, the rhythm of Newtown...where the largest number of persons congregated.

Lanza's obsessive mind took in his experiences and surroundings in a centripetal process like an eddy ensnaring and distorting and eventually transmuting these utterly as it was pulled toward the center point of stark madness. This process was unnoticed by and unrecognizable to anyone with a hint of rationality. Progressing outside of the principles and contours of rationality, in accordance with its subtleties and deviousness, it was destroying whatever rationality Adam Lanza may have had and the restraints going with this.

Lanza's exterior was quiet, passive, withdrawn; so he has been described. Such traits were the perimeter for the turbulence within; like the contours of a vessel which not only keeps some liquid within, but also holds the ambient surroundings out. Living in Newtown since he was six when his family moved there from New Hampshire and attending town schools and although he was a loner inevitably becoming familiar with much of Newtown in the normal course of life, Lanza absorbed Newtown. Estranged as he was and as hostile as he became, it wasn't these aberrations that brought him to the murders at the elementary school. Lanza never had a developed enough concept of community to become hostile to Newtown as a community. A Newtown target was chosen because Newtown was practically everything he had ever been exposed to to become obsessive about.

To his demented mind and monstrously perverse sense of values, it would make no sense if the murders did not have at least a blush of intimacy. Adam Lanza could not kill complete strangers, or he would be seen as a madman. This does not mean that he killed the children as a way of "explaining" himself to others; so that others would finally know him. Lanza did not act out of the intent to leave a legacy, an indelible reminder of him, that he had lived. He committed murder where and how he did because of dark forces at work within him insidiously dissolving his person (or self) while allowing him to believe that he was maintaining this person and satisfactorily had control primarily as volition over it.

Lanza's withdrawn demeanor was an unintentional, biological, disguise for stymieing others in detecting, at the most barely sensing at all what was occurring psychically, organically, physiologically within him. For Lanza himself, the withdrawal and passivity were frustrations like pressures complicating his condition--or attributes--so he was preoccupied to the point of disabling him from any realization of his own slipping into the heart of darkness and thus any resistance to or movement from it if only some signs of appealing for help.

5. Assault

Despite the severe and eventual murderous psychic tumult and displacement, Lanza retained an irrefrangible lucidity in his innermost, inaccessible self, little different from an instinct. Where it differed from sheer instinct was in summoning a logic to devise the best plan for the contemplated deadly deed and the required steps for carrying it out; like a lion singles out its victim in a herd of zebra by recognizing its slowness, youth, infirmity, or some other characteristic marking it good prey. Wanting his plan to be a success, Lanza's untethered lucidity and aberrant logic worked to devise a plan to maximize the chances for this.

Sandy Hook Elementary School had been singled out. The occupants of the firehouse posed no deterrent. There were probably people going in and out of Dickenson Road all day. A lone driver in a common compact car (a black Honda Civic) could be the brother or sister of one of the students or a son or daughter of one of the school employees coming to pick her up or drop something off. The elementary school was an easily-accessible public building with varied levels of activity going on in relation to it all day.

Accessibility and approachability were not the only concerns however. Surprise with its inevitable effects of confusion and disorientation if only for a moment was an important element of the plan too. Surprise is always an advantage for the predator, as the lion creeping up on its prey. Dickenson Drive conduced to this in that once past the firehouse, there was nothing else along the road; and furthermore--the best of all--between Dickenson and the school was a wooded area thick enough so that even in winter, the approach of a car would be obscured. Past the wooded area, Dickenson curved taking a car out of view of the firehouse; and it opened up into a parking lot. There was a baseball diamond to the left, and across from this the paved parking lot began. One runs beside it for only a short distance, a few seconds at most, and then turns right into the main area of the parking lot where during hours when school is open, you pass along a double row of parked cars to your left.

It would be slightly quicker to get to the front entrance to not follow the traffic pattern of the lot indicated by large arrows drawn on the pavement by going to the left of the double row of parked cars. But doing this one might attract attention taking away from the intended surprise. One would be driving right by the first-grade classrooms at one's left that were going to be the primary target of the assault. First-graders and their teachers might be looking out on the assailant driving the wrong way through the parking lot, and an alert might go out to the office that someone who didn't know about the parking-lot rules or didn't care to observe them was coming up to the school. After months and likely years of maintaining an inscrutable exterior, Adam Lanza would not want to have this fall away by going the wrong way in a one-way lane.

So Lanza took the right at the double row of parked cars. This was a little longer way to the front entrance with the glass doors, but the double row of parked cars which would then be between his car and the school, like the wooded area a moment earlier, would help to obscure his approach.

Coming to the end of the double row of parked cars, the parking-lot lane makes a u-turn toward the school. The approach to the school from this angle is a blind spot. A brick wall with no windows faces out on this part of the parking-lot lane to the front entrance. "Sandy Hook Elementary" is written along this wall. Lanza pulled up near the left end of the wall (as one faces it) and parked outside of a fire lane marked by yellow stripes inside a yellow border. Newscast aerial views of the scene show where he parked his car facing the front doors not far away now at a forty-five degree angle.

To this point, Lanza was probably still unobserved; or if he had been observed, he had shown nothing out of the ordinary. Getting out of his car dressed in a black pullover, military cargo pants, and the utility vest filled with ammunition and carrying a rifle, he probably still remained unobserved. At the spot where he had parked the Civic, the brick wall with no windows and the school name juts out; and where Lanza parked he was still short of having driven by the entrance--which would have taken him into view from one or more classrooms--when the car might have been spotted by someone in the office or in the long corridor onto which the glass doors at the entrance opened to. It's unlikely alarm would have been raised had the car been seen; but at the least, someone would know there was a car out front with the likelihood that someone would be coming to the entrance shortly.

Getting this close unobserved, it was now only a few quick strides to the glass front doors which could be easily blown out with the high-powered weapons Lanza was now armed with. He was familiar enough with the school to know that even if the doors were locked, he could quickly gain entry. Having gotten unobserved or virtually unnoticed this close and now free from the car and heavily armed, there was nothing that could stop him.

The first action Adam Lanza did in his assault was shoot out the glass window of one of the doors. He may have reached in to grab a handle to pull open the door or gotten through the broken glass. Wearing the utility vest of rugged material and underneath this, a military-style black pullover, he could have pushed his way through any remaining shards of glass without injuring himself or slowing down the assault.

Lanza was inside quickly enough so that his primary weapon the semiautomatic Bushmaster XM-15 rifle was ready for use. As the school principal Dawn Hochsprung and school psychologist Mary Sherlach rushed toward him out of a meeting with some of the school's teachers, Lanza shot them dead. His next steps are unclear because by now, the school was going into defensive measures teachers and other staff had been taught. Someone in the principal's office had switched on the microphone of the intercom system connected to all the classrooms. If teachers had not heard the gunfire breaking out near the front doors, the sound of shouts and gunfire coming over the intercom system alerted them. Whatever the details of the beginnings of the assault with individuals coming out of the principal's office or near it, besides the two dead, two other adults were wounded as Lanza fired more shots in this area.

The school nurse Sarah Cox reports that from under her desk where she had hidden upon hearing the gunshots, she saw Lanza's lower legs and boots when he opened the door and stared in for a few seconds. Evidence shows that there is no doubt that Lanza spent a brief moment--a fraction of a minute--in the vicinity of the principle's office firing into it and checking an adjacent office, presumably to try to prevent an alert from going outside of the school. An aspect of my theory of why Lanza killed his mother in her bedroom was to be sure she would not raise any alarm if upon leaving her bedroom, she found that he and also some of her licensed guns were missing. As carefully planned as the assault was, short as it turned out to be, and as long as it had been brewing, he would have taken care that it was not interrupted before its aim of the killings went into effect by his mother alarmed over his absence. Similarly, Lanza wouldn't want his aim interfered with by staff in or near the office overpowered him or sending out an alarm. Shooting down a couple and frightening the others so they would not come out of where they had sought safety, Lanza felt he could now go to the classrooms which were his ultimate destination for the groups of helpless victims he would find there.

The cafeteria/auditorium to Lanza's right when he broke into the front entrance was a possible ready target area. As reported, there were children in there practicing a holiday program. The cafeteria/auditorium was large however, and would have had exits to adjoining rooms and to outside. Lanza would not have complete dominance of the space. He didn't want to be hunting down fleeing children and teachers, nor having to spend time getting close to individuals or groups around the large space for close-range, well-aimed shots with the increased probability of being deadly.

Besides, volleys of shots coming from the cafeteria/auditorium would alert others not already aware of the threat and also give ones already alerted more time to barricade, hide, or flee to defend themselves.

From the vicinity of the office after the brief moment he had spent focused on it, Lanza went to the long corridor to his left as he entered the school. This was where the kindergarten and first-grade classrooms were. These were on the left. On the right was a row of four classrooms for other grades; three and then the fourth on the other side of a narrow hallway leading to more classrooms and then the media center.

The greatest carnage took place in the first-grade classroom of teacher Lauren Rousseau. How Lanza got into the classroom has not yet been reported. But by the time he was finished here, 14 students ages six and seven lay dead with their teacher.

Teacher Victoria Soto's adjacent classroom was the next target area. When Lanza entered, students of hers hidden in a closet and cupboards panicked, and came out and tried to run through the door. Six were killed. Law-enforcement investigators are still trying to find out what happened in the fear and confusion. According to (unconfirmed) reports from some of the surviving children of Soto's class, there was a lull in the shooting at this point apparently from Lanza's rifle jamming or him having to reload by putting another clip in, perhaps dropping this or fumbling with it. At some point, Lanza killed Victoria Soto. Six children from her classroom did manage to escape, and fled to a nearby house where the owner took them in and kept them occupied until first responders took them to their parents later.

Lanza's shooting spree was coming to an end. No more now than earlier did he want to be chasing fleeing, dispersing children or leave himself vulnerable to attack from individuals or ones banding together from different directions in a place he was only generally familiar with. Lanza felt comfortable enough in the confines of a classroom where he was in complete control by having small children and teachers terrified as he wielded a semiautomatic rifle with two handguns in reserve and loads of more ammunition. It was like being at the target range his mother had taken him to several or more times. Helpless, weak, scared young children huddled in one part of the classroom were like targets at the range. They were almost lifeless like the targets in that they would not attack him. Once any adults who presented resistance were taken care of, Lanza was in the zone he had darkly dreamed of where he was an all-powerful demiurge deciding on the life or death of others.

But with the lull in the shooting from whatever glitch arose with the rifle and the children escaping out the door, the universe of the classroom filled at once with tumult and the fluid, soothing exercise of total dominance was lost. The plan was coming apart.

The total dominance--unrivaled and self-created--couldn't last forever. But that it was created and lasted for a short while was enough, enough for a lifetime. It was the pinnacle of a lifetime of 20 years. Adam Lanza did not want to go back. He had done much to destroy anything he could have gone back to. The sirens of first responders had gotten more shrill by the second. Commotion in the hallway near the front doors, the place he had entered the school and from which he had made his way to the classrooms, would be armed first responders searching out the intruder.

Lanza was glimpsed by one of them. He was seen momentarily in the hallway outside of Soto's room, then ducked back into it. Lanza saw or knew from the commotion that first responders among whom would be armed police officers were closing in. In the hallway outside of Soto's classroom, he must have thought of trying to make it to another classroom--one more classroom--for more killing. But the impulse quickly vanished. Lanza took the few steps to go back into Soto's classroom, the site where he had fleetingly enjoyed the exercise of ultimate power and unquestionable validation. He would know that this site was not a site of refuge or remove. Nonetheless it was appealing and comfortable, like an answer.

Seconds after ducking back into Soto's classroom where victims were strewn, Adam Lanza shot himself in the head with one of the handguns he had been carrying in his cargo pants.

6. The Murdered Mother

An hour or more earlier, Lanza had killed his mother in her bed by shooting her multiple times in the face. A reconstruction of the timeline indicates that Nancy Lanza could have been shot no later than about 9:00AM for Adam Lanza to have gotten to Sandy Hook Elementary School by about 9:30AM, the time estimated within a couple of minutes when he broke out the glass of a locked front door and entered the school. This is the timeline that has been reconstructed by law-enforcement officials and given to the media. Based on the times of recorded 911 calls from the school and calls to first responders prompted by these, this timeline can change only in incidental ways with ongoing investigation. For example, the precise time Lanza entered the school through the broken glass may be determined. But this will not vary much from the estimated 9:30AM time, and will not change the sequence of events inside the school as pieced together from survivors' accounts and forensic evidence of bullet holes, shell casings, and distribution of bodies.

Lacking medical or factual evidence to specify the time of Nancy Lanza's murder, official reports, as they typically are in the absence of demonstrable foundation, will be conservative and general. Regarding the murder of Nancy Lanza, such reports will presumably state something along the lines "no later than about 9:00AM." This is a reasonable public report concerning the mother's murder--and also safe so as not to stir controversy--in that it allows Adam Lanza time to accomplish one or more of the several actions he unarguably did accomplish as inferred by physical evidence at the school, the site of the shootings. For instance, Adam Lanza had to gather the large amount of ammunition found in his cargo pants and pockets of the fishing vest. He had to collect the four guns he brought to the school, the three he carried into the school with him and the fourth found in the trunk of his mother's car parked near the school's front entrance.

Law-enforcement officials and others associated with them have to allow some time for Adam Lanza to do the tasks at his home he plainly had to do and then drive to the school to be there by about 9:30AM; thus estimating the time of the mother's death at about 9:00AM. However, considering other factors which law-enforcement officials and ones working with them would typically regard as speculative--and necessarily so considering their official responsibilities and credibility entailing legal requirements of proof--I think the time of Nancy Lanza's murder can be presumed to be between 7:00AM and 8:00AM, probably closer to the end of this hour. My grounds for giving this earlier timeframe are common morning habits in many homes, Nancy Lanza's personality as sketchily described by people who knew her, varied specific acts Adam Lanza did before leaving the home for the school, and Lanza's methodical plotting extending much beyond the home but including it regarding what he saw he had to do to give his ultimate aim of mass murder at Sandy Hook Elementary School the best chances for succeeding.

Beginning with common morning habits, most individuals are out of bed by 9:00AM. Neighbors and friends who knew her describe Nancy Lanza as active and social. She doesn't seem like the type who would sleep late or linger in bed long after awakening. She had certain documented habits such as socializing with neighbors at the end of the day for a glass of wine or having a meal at a local bar/restaurant called "My Place." Although there are some reports that Nancy Lanza expressed concern over Adam and was thinking about changes she thought might help him, no one reports that she looked outwardly drawn, defeated, or undone by whatever was going on with him or between them. Although she was troubled by her son's condition, she occasionally went on brief vacations back to New Hampshire where she was from to visit relatives and according to one news item I saw, went not long before with her other son Ryan to New Orleans for a concert. As worried and probably to some degree upset as she was over her mystifying son Adam, there is no evidence that she was lethargic or depressed from this.

Knowing his mother's habits and nature, Adam Lanza knew she would not still be in bed as late as 9:00AM. If she were in bed as late as 9:00AM because Adam Lanza knew she habitually was or I am wrong she was in the habit of being up earlier, Adam nonetheless could not take the chance that she might be up and around the house. He had too much to do before leaving for the school, and he didn't want to be interrupted or distracted by thinking about or keeping tabs on her free and thus unpredictable movement in the house. The mother's worry, suspicions, or questions about Adam Lanza's systematic, untoward actions could be enough to throw off the plan. At least, they would be distracting. A solitary, inward person, Lanza worked best when he was alone, as when playing his video games. His unfolding plans for the rest of the morning required utmost concentration and focus.

Worst of all, his mother would sound an alarm bringing the planned massacre to an end before it started. The mother had to be killed, and early, before she got out of her bed. This was critical for the plan to get off on the right foot. As with the school children, the mother was to be caught by surprise and in as vulnerable as situation as possible for the shooting. Groups of small children in the confines of a classroom with Lanza heavily armed and standing by the only doorway was the desirable situation at the school. At home, the mother sleeping was the most desirable situation.

Lanza shot his mother several times (the news I heard is four times) in the face as she was laying in her bed. One presumes she was still sleeping. Whether she was sleeping or not, the prime detail for analysis is that she had the covers pulled up over nearly all her body leaving her head out.

Law-enforcement, FBI, and other investigators presume and remark publicly that shootings in the face of the victim, especially multiple times, indicates a rage or hatred against the victim; a violent attempt to efface the victim so to speak. This is what seems to be supposed in this case according to limited, mostly casual, comments by officials and media consultants in short interviews who have had anything to say beyond the fact of the mother's death by multiple gunshots to the face. However, as I see it, the motive of rage or hatred in the mother's death is mistaken. If Adam Lanza were going to kill his mother out of rage or hatred, he probably would have done this earlier. In sleeping in her bed for many hours and presumably motionless or near so, Nancy Lanza could not have been doing anything to ignite rage in Adam Lanza. Adam Lanza was armed when he went to her bedroom to murder her. He had the intention of killing her even before he came to her bedroom. Not long after he shot her, he left for the school. Killing the mother was part of the overall plan, not an act provoked by specific rage or hatred.

Nancy Lanza was shot in the face because her face was the only part of her exposed as she was laying motionless in bed. Shooting at her still face, Adam Lanza could be sure he had hit her. He could see the mortal wounds he was inflicting. As with the children and probably the school principal and psychologist and other adults too, Nancy Lanza was shot multiple times because Adam Lanza wanted to be sure she was dead; he wanted to be sure he accomplished what he meant to accomplish.

Shooting the large majority of the victims multiple times was an element in the thoroughness of Lanza's planning and the demiurgic willfulness in which he carried it out. He sought finality, not random mayhem and carnage. Except for the appearance of the school principal and psychologist rushing out of the main office at the sounds of the shots breaking the front-door glass, Lanza came upon his victims in a situation where the probability of this finality was maximized. His victims could not run away. Whether the motionless mother in her bedroom or the frail schoolchildren cringing in a corner with only one or two adults to try to guard over them, Lanza had his victims in a situation where he could shoot each multiple times, increasing the chance each would be dead with each shot. According to his planning, the targeted victims would be shot at close range, increasing the chances even more. At close range, not only would his shots be more accurate, but he would be able to determine if they had been effective. Soft moans, small movements, barely audible breathing, a trace of life left in an eye, or other signs of remaining life would not be detected except at close range. Close range along with the strength of the weapons, mainly the semiautomatic rifle, and amount of ammunition combined with vulnerable, virtually trapped, targets were all factors of Adam Lanza's planning to make sure his actions wreaked the finality he sought.

Shooting someone in the face is not invariably an indication of extreme rage and hatred. Hit men and assassins, for example, shoot into the faces of their targets because this is an open, vulnerable area and close to the brain. Shots to the face are sure to do serious damage; and multiple shots to the face hitting eyes or temples will almost certainly kill a target. Shots to the face at the mouth or jaw or cheeks will do serious damage; and if missing the brain, will fracture the upper spine--i. e., the neck--causing incapacitating or eventually fatal injuries. Professional killers, hit men and assassins have no animosity toward their targets. They are detached. Adam Lanza, too, was probably detached in killing his mother; as the timing and pattern of the following shootings at the school were methodical indicating a detached, purposeful, controlled manner of shooting.

The determination and deadliness of the mass shootings at the school at first confused experienced first responders. Realizing the numbers of persons shot, first responders called for ambulances and alerted Danbury Hospital to be prepared for multiple casualties. Ambulances were sent to the school, and at the Hospital readied four emergency rooms and six operating rooms to receive casualties upon being notified of shootings at a school in Newtown a little after 10:00AM. However, only three of the ambulances were needed--for two wounded children and a wounded adult. The children died at the hospital. The rest of the ambulances were soon sent away after first responders realized they would not be needed. The three ambulances arrived one after the other at the Hospital about 10:30AM. Doctors and nurses at the hospital waited for more. But none came. About noon, the Hospital received a second call saying that there would be no more ambulances. By this time or sooner, first responders and medical professionals and law-enforcement investigators arriving soon after them had had time to check the many children and few adults who had been shot and were laying in the two classrooms plus the school principal and psychologist laying in the hall outside of the main office. All were dead. One girl child who had been in teacher Victoria Soto's classroom escaped alive by having the presence of mind to play dead among the bodies grouped around and on top of her. By then, she had left the school covered with blood to join her mother where parents were gathered not far from the school.

Adam Lanza's determined and directed ferocity at first escaped professional, experienced first responders, most of whom were

local and state police on whose heels came FBI and ATF agents.
Just as investigating officials failed to initially grasp what they
came upon at the school, so could they fail to grasp what Nancy
Lanza's mortal face wounds indicated about Adam Lanza's state of
mind and intent regarding this murder.

7. The Perfect Crime

After killing his mother, sure she was dead by multiple gunshots to
her face at close range, Adam Lanza went about completing tasks
in preparation for the coming surprise assault on the school. With
his mother dead, he could concentrate on these with no concern
about interruption.

The mother was killed with one of her high-powered rifles. Adam
Lanza did not take this rifle to the school. Instead he took another
rifle, a semiautomatic Bushmaster .223, a shotgun, and two
handguns, a SIG Sauer 9mm and a Glock 9mm. The Bushmaster
was a slightly modified civilian version of the military M-16 rifle;
which is also used by many law-enforcement agencies. The two
handguns were types favored by many police officers. Adam
Lanza did not bring the shotgun into the school with him. Police
found it in the trunk of the mother's car parked near the school
front entrance when going through it after the massacre and
Lanza's suicide.

Investigators have not said yet where the rifle Lanza used to kill
his mother was found. Lanza may have left it near or in her
bedroom, he may have returned it to its place where the mother
kept her guns in the furnished basement; he may have left Ito

anywhere in the house. Police were able to find it however, and determine that it was the gun used to kill Nancy Lanza.

In my plausible tracing of Adam Lanza's movements after shooting his mother in her bedroom, I have him going down to the basement, taking the rifle for the killing with him. I heard one report--not see since by me and apparently not widely circulated--that police investigating the Yogananda Street house where Nancy and Adam Lanza lived found Adam Lanza's bedroom in perfect order (presumably the upstairs bedroom which he may not have used much). The report mentioned that police who had entered Adam Lanza's room found clothes neatly, seemingly painstakingly, folded. The newscaster relating what she had learned about what the police had come upon in Adam Lanza's bedroom in a tone of surprise, presumably meaning to convey not only what the police saw in the bedroom, but how they reacted to this. The newscaster did not mention anything else but the carefully folded clothing. One assumes this was all the police mentioned to exemplify the exceptionally neatly-kept bedroom; which they regarded as an anomaly they reacted to with surprise bordering on amazement. Though only the clothing was noted, that police thought what they had seen worth relating and the implications of the tone in which the newscaster related it, one goes on to assume that anything on a dresser or table was not strewn, but similarly neatly arranged; any shirts on hangers in a closet did not droop to one side or another, but appeared regimented; shoes were aligned; socks were not loose, but neatly arranged in pairs, or if rolled into one another in pairs, the pairs were neatly arranged like eggs in a carton. In short, there was nothing casual about the room.

As was conveyed by the newscaster's tone, the police saw the neatness of the room anomalous. The newscaster ended her short report by saying that the police said they found the neatness of Adam Lanza's room anomalous because who bothers to make sure their room is so neat when he is going to commit suicide before long anyway? Adam Lanza's neatness however is organically connected to his shooting his victims multiple times to make sure they were dead. It was more so this than rage or hatred which accounts for the multiple shots to each victim. Neatness is a type of finality. Lanza no more wanted his victims to have any life in them than he wanted his shirts, shoes, bedroom furnishings, etc. to be out of order in the slightest. For him, the certainty of murder was like making sure his clothing was neatly folded and stored.

Certainly dead victims and the neatest possible bedroom alike were actions he took giving him a sense of control in his cloistered, circumscribed world; which control, like the control he had in the video games he played, was to him a major part of the diminished, unusual life he had in him. And the control also gave him feedback which was a primary source of affirmation that there was life within him. This is a major part of the inner dialogue going on with Lanza; which repetitively over considerable time created for him a removed self that eventually, terribly, was coherent and trusted enough to plan and carry out mass murder.

At least from when Lanza was in the Newtown High School technology club in the early years of high school about 2007 before his mother took him out of school, he had been playing computer games. Club members would have parties in various homes where they would enthusiastically play computer games. Interest in computers and playing computer games didn't stop there for Lanza. In the basement of the Yogananda Street home, there was a computer where he could play games as much as he wanted.

One of the members of the high-school tech club said Lanza liked to play violent video games especially. Comfortably furnished not only with the computer, but also a bed and TV and with a bathroom, the basement was a second bedroom for Lanza where he apparently spent most of his time alone playing video games. The basement is also the place said to be where Nancy Lanza stored the five weapons she had legally purchased and registered. The day of the massacre, the plan may have started to unfold from this basement bedroom. Adam Lanza may have stayed in the basement the night before where he would be near the gun for shooting his mother. This would not raise any suspicions since he must have spent the night there regularly. And it would be more efficient not having to go down to the basement to get the gun in the morning; or otherwise risk being discovered by his mother bringing the rifle to his other bedroom. Being in the basement near the guns would also be better because there would be no risk, however small, that he might wake his mother in the morning going down to get a gun. Recognizing that Lanza's thoughtful planning considered having his mother as unaware and helpless as possible suggests that the basement was the best place for him to begin putting the plan in motion.

Besides the comment reported from police by the newscaster about the extraordinary neatness of Lanza's room which seems to have become lost in the volume of reporting on the massacre, there is one other detail which has been videotaped and much shown, but not received any comment so far as I know. The videotape is the one where Adam Lanza's mother's car, a black Honda Civic, is parked in front of Sandy Hook Elementary School near the front entrance where he shot out the glass of a door so he could get inside. This detail is that in parking the car, Adam Lanza kept it outside of the yellow-striped, no-parking fire lane. As videotapes taken from news channel helicopters hovering overhead show, the car is parked right at the edge of the striped fire lane. It is parked in a spot where it cannot be seen from anywhere inside the school except a small area near the front door, and then only if someone is looking out for something around the corner of the part of the school jutting out a little near where the car was parked.

Like Adam Lanza's carefully folded clothes which appeared to be an anomaly for the police officers searching the house on Yogananda Street, Adam Lanza's parking the car outside of the fire lane evidences a sense of order and observance of simple laws for the public good, as simple habits of neatness contribute to personal well-being. Although the car was parked where it was hard to see from anyone inside the school, and even then an individual would have to be looking out from a small area where no individual would normally be standing, if Lanza did pull into the fire lane closer to the wall of the part of the school jutting out with the name Sandy Hook Elementary School written on it, the car would have been impossible by anyone to see from any spot in the school.

As meticulous as Lanza's planning for the assault had been with particular attention on surprise and not having it be interrupted at any point before he could close in on his victims in the classrooms, one could think that he would have by plan or instinct pulled the mother's car he was driving closer to the school into the fire lane to be certain of being unobserved at this critical point of the instant before he was to break into the school to reach his ultimate objective. And yet, Lanza parks the car right at the edge of the fire lane, where anyone planning to be in and out of the school quickly in dropping something off in the front office not far from the entrance, for example, would park. The preciseness with which Lanza parked the car is another small detail in the many details involved in the massacre which are coming to light. I see it, like the neatness of his bedroom, as disclosing Lanza's dissociative state. He parked the car in a spot where it looks as if he thought he would be coming back to it, after he went inside the school to take care of what he had come for, thereby fixing some things he felt were wrong with his world.

Neat and well-organized as he was, Adam Lanza probably would have wanted to return the rifle he took upstairs to shoot his mother to its place in the basement. This would be the natural thing for him to do anyway since he would be going down to the basement to get the three guns he wanted to take to the school. Also in the basement were the computer hard drives he would destroy. The black pullover and cargo pants and the utility vest with many pockets for holding ammunition were probably in the basement bedroom too. At some point, Lanza got dressed in these. The ammunition he wanted to take to the school for the guns he was going to use presumably was stored near the guns.

8. Destroying the Hard Drive

Lanza had a variety of tasks to do before leaving for the school. I don't think he would have got started on these or completed them before killing his mother. This makes her killing seem like only another one of the preparatory tasks. He wanted to kill his mother because he wanted to make sure she would not interrupt his preparations and possibly sound an alarm by calling 911 or fleeing to a neighbor's house. Or she might even get into her car to flee or if alive, take it for an errand. Adam Lanza could not afford to let anything like this happen.

Shooting the mother when she was shot in the planned sequence of events was a least as much a practical measure as it was a psychic event. As emotionally deadened as Adam Lanza was, it is seen as basically the practical measure; whereas seeing it as a psychic event ascribes it to the category of matricide as symbolic or gets psychologically theoretical about it. There is no doubt that the killing of the mother left Adam Lanza free to go about his tasks of the morning without having to be concerned about being interrupted. Investigators say Adam Lanza left no notes. They have found no written evidence of his intention to commit massacre. A list of tasks to do before leaving the house on that morning would be one such piece of written evidence. No list has been found. With the thoroughness of the planning so as not to be prematurely exposed or interrupted at any step, Adam Lanza had to have thought his plan out in detail over a period of time. He probably did some scouting too along the route he planned and at the school he planned to assault. Adam Lanza had the plan in his mind. He was not one to make notes, keep a journal, work on a novel, or do other kinds of written activities. He can be imagined to be running over in his mind each step of his plan in the hours leading up to its outbreak with the taking of the rifle and going out of the basement to quietly move through the house to his mother's bedroom to kill her.

Killing the mother as the first step makes logical sense more than it does sense psychically or psychologically; although either of these cannot be kept out for amplified understanding of Adam Lanza and events of the day of the massacre. If Lanza had been living with a roommate, he probably would have killed him for the same practical reasons he killed his mother. The shooting of the mother thereby removing any possible means of interruption at least in the early stages assured that the plan maintained its cogency, including the several tasks to be done in the basement, and acquired the right momentum.

One of the other tasks to be done in the basement was destroying the hard drive of the computer he used to play the video games. One investigator has been quoted as describing this as "expertly destroyed." (It has also been reported that Lanza destroyed the hard drive of an Xbox or some such device for playing video games, although there was no evidence he used this for game-playing; which would have required registration including a credit-card number. The hard drive referred to in my discussion is the drive of the desktop or similar basement computer Lanza used when playing the video games.) Lanza patently understood well not only how to use a computer as indicated by his hours of playing video games, but also the hardware running the computer. One member of Lanza's high-school computer club said he could take a computer apart and put it back together in minutes. Lanza became deeply drawn to computers; and in his insular life, computers took on an outsized and central place. Speaking of the destroyed computer hard drive, FBI and other commentators have said it was so knowledgeably destroyed that they may never get anything off of it.

I have not heard where the destroyed hard drive was found. This may give some clue as to Lanza's motive in destroying it, although I doubt this. The time when he destroyed the hard drive--which presumably there is no way to determine--might also give a clue to motive. But I doubt this too. Apart from the always significant question of motive for a crime--which is unlikely to ever be specified or finalized in this case--the time when Lanza destroyed the computer drive would help in trying to imagine the length of time, the direction or orientation, and the valence or gestalt of Lanza's state of mind. Especially, the time of Lanza's destruction of the hard drive in relation to the time when he killed his mother could be informative to such questions about state of mind.

In keeping with my intuitions and reasoning about the sequence of events Lanza took the day of the massacre seeing the shooting of the mother as the initiating action (considering the selection of the rifle for this in the basement as incidental, as relevant as this is to intention), I think Lanza destroyed the hard drive after killing his mother, as easy as this would have been for him at any time with his knowledge of computers and ability to take one apart and reassemble it. Given the pattern and cogency of the overall plan, it doesn't seem that he would begin tasks in the basement, such as destroying the hard drive, then take the rifle and go shoot his mother, then return to the basement to resume the tasks. The first order of business after a night of reviewing the plan was to kill the mother. She was the one unpredictable element in the house which could interfere with his long-brewing, carefully-thought-out plan which was to be carried out on this day.

There was no chance that any other person would come to the house to interfere with the part of the plan being done there by postponing it by Lanza having to interact with the individual in any way or possibly ruin the plan by detecting something and sounding an alarm. In recent years, there is no information on anyone being in the house besides Adam Lanza and his mother. The father lived in Stamford, Connecticut; and the brother Ryan lived in Hoboken, New Jersey. They both had well-paying, responsible jobs; and they would be working on the Friday. Moreover, Adam Lanza had cut off contact with both of them a couple of years earlier. Knowing this and also knowing her son's inscrutable, moody, fragile condition, Nancy Lanza would surely have told Adam if either of them were coming to the house that morning; although this is a theoretical point since the possibility of either doing this was nil. That either would be not going to work the Friday morning, come a good distance to get to the house, and disrespect Adam's overt desire not to have contact with them is inconceivable.

Neighbors say that Nancy Lanza was sociable and fairly active outside her house. She visited neighbors for afternoon glasses of wine, and attended game nights in nearby neighbors' homes. She obviously interacted regularly with neighbors. Neighbors do not say, however, that she had invited them into her home for wine or games in recent years. There is nothing strange about this though since many people like to get out after spending most of their time indoors in their home. Nancy Lanza was also a regular at the Newtown bar/restaurant called My Place; another place she liked to get out to.

In retrospect now after the massacre, one gathers that Nancy Lanza had other reasons for not having people into her home. She was trying to shelter Adam from contact which other people which she knew caused disturbances in him. At the same time, she was keeping others from coming into contact with Adam because she knew his behavior or demeanor might disturb them. Trying to keep her home as a zone where whatever was affecting her son would not be aggravated and might be ameliorated was not a complex, secretive strategy Nancy Lanza was employing, but simply an act of consideration for all concerned. Whatever problems Adam had, they were her problems, not the neighbors', the friends' and acquaintances' at My Place, nor the landscapers'. A landscaper doing work regularly at the Lanza Yogananda Street house interviewed a day or two after the massacre told the anecdote of Nancy Lanza bringing a rifle she wanted him to see out to the yard, not asking him into the house to see it. The landscaper said he thought this was a little unusual. What I see as the only element of this incident worth commenting on is that Nancy Lanza wanted the landscaper to see the rifle, not that she didn't ask the landscaper into the house. I don't know why Nancy Lanza would care one way or another if the landscaper knew she had the rifle, or that she was a gun enthusiast. And I don't know anything about interchanges between the two when the landscaper was doing work at the house. The reason I see Nancy Lanza bringing the rifle outside for the landscaper to see goes along with her habit--which may have become reflexive by the time of this incident--and developed disposition of engaging with others outside of the house.

Adam Lanza must have known in living in the house for years that with his mother gone, there was virtually no chance that any other person would be about to interfere with the plan. Intense, absorbed, and preoccupied as he was, Lanza would not want to be distracted in the tasks he wanted to get done in the basement.

In the scenario I'm drawing, Lanza's first task after killing his mother was destroying the hard drive. The tasks were sequenced so that Lanza would undergo a transformation so he would be hardly recognizable to himself, as much as he had any introspection or self-consciousness required for doing this. As madness is a condition entailing the loss of all restraint except as deception and camouflage, the descent into madness entails the shedding of any remaining inhibitions or constraints so what was being obscured both in oneself and to others by deception and camouflage becomes present immediately--unmediated--in all its terrible rawness. In the descent into madness, the individual does not come to know one's true self, but becomes bereft of any sources or references for any self. In the sequence of tasks in the early part of the plan, Adam Lanza was distancing himself from himself to the point where not even an echo of his regular self enabling him to get from day to day, however unreliable, tormenting, or painful this self might be, was left. Lanza was imperceptibly, gradually but certainly, succumbing to madness, becoming the madman.

Although to Adam Lanza's now-warped mind past the point of return, the mother was killed because the plan required this as a practical first step in order to give it the best possible chance for being fulfilled by eliminating any possibility of early detection, as progression of the plan in its early stages in the house--i. e., tasks to be done there--concerned shedding inhibitions while at the same time retaining and as required, creating enough of a framework of agency to function. The sequence of Lanza's tasks, points along the way to utter madness, were forming an unrecognizable, yet functioning entity. Once past the point of no return, all there was was only a functioning entity, a perfected functioning entity.

The murder of the mother as the first practical step toward the fulfillment of the plan cannot be separated out of the killing of the mother as a necessary step in the change to unadulterated madness. Lanza used a rifle to kill the mother. But given his state of mind as can be reasonably assessed and the acts he did commit, it does not seem plausible that Lanza would have sought out his mother to kill if she had been away from the house and there were no possibility that she would interfere with his actions. There are reports however that for about three days before the day of the massacre, Nancy Lanza was in New Hampshire on a brief vacation. Bretton Woods in mid-state New Hampshire is given as a location she was known to be at. From New Hampshire with relatives living there, she may have stopped other places too. Adam Lanza probably waited until she returned. When Nancy Lanza would be away from the house for a few days on one of her periodic short vacations usually to New Hampshire, she would leave meals for Adam (so news reports say). She would surely tell Adam when she expected to be back. Adam may have waited until she returned from this brief stay in New Hampshire because he knew in the perverted way one slipping into madness knows she had to be murdered for the transformation his madness was seeking to take place.

After the mother's murder which I estimated between 7:00AM and 8:00AM, the next step would be destroying the hard drive. This might have been done when Adam was alone when his mother was away in New Hampshire. But my scenario of the act of madness on the day of the massacre, especially the cogency and direction of the act as partly deduced and partly intuited from a grasp of Adam Lanza's state of mind and mental processes as much as this can be glimpsed, does not support this conjecture. For destroying the hard drive while the mother was away in New Hampshire in the few days preceding the massacre would mean taking the computer apart to get to the hard drive, and then putting it back together with the destroyed hard drive missing so the mother would not suspect anything was awry, or going awry, in seeing the disassembled or tampered with computer. Besides, Adam Lanza would not want to have deprived himself from using the computer to play the video games which were his main source of skewed enjoyment and sensation and slim link to a world of others beyond himself. Along with the mother's murder, destroying the hard drive would have been one of the first acts Lanza in the process of becoming crazed, though in this nonetheless remaining controlled, would have done in initiating his plan. Killing his mother and destroying the hard drive of his computer were acts on the same plane of finality which were concomitantly cutting himself off from everything of his previous life and entering into the strange, ineluctable world of madness. In this passage, the guns, familiar objects from his previous life, would take on new, warped uses as instruments of madness.

First responders found out that Adam Lanza lived at or had some association with the Yogananda Street house from finding the brother Ryan's identification paper on Adam Lanza's body. Other law-enforcement agencies were immediately notified, and local and state police rushed to the house. Their first entry into the house was the standard police procedure of gaining control over what was assumed to be the origin of the terrible violence at the school (with the remote possibility of breaking up the plans of other plotters still at the house, as New Jersey police out of an abundance of caution arrested the brother Ryan in Hoboken). Upon securing the location, the first police responders according to procedure would have turned to making sure anything which might be used as evidence for solving the crime or revealing motive is preserved. This step is basically not touching, moving, or analyzing anything so the crime-scene investigators to follow trained in gathering and labeling evidence by means of removal, photographs, or onsite analysis can do their work with the scene as undisturbed as possible. In their actions to secure the Yogananda

Street House and while waiting for the crime-scene investigators, first police responders would be noting various articles or phenomena (e. g., blood stains, objects that looked out of place) to report to the crime-scene investigators.

In the case of the first-responders to the Lanza Yogananda Street house when their presence turned from crime prevention to preliminary investigation concerned with identifying and securing in place anything they were able to see which might be evidence, they discovered Nancy Lanza's body in her bedroom. Since like the mother's body and also the extraordinary neatness of Adam Lanza's bedroom coming out in the early hours of the unfolding of the media coverage, the destruction of the hard drive must have been something that was conveyed from officials on the basis of what had been observed at the house by first-responders or following investigators in the first stages of the formal, methodical investigation.

Presumably in the basement, first-responders to the Yogananda Street house would have seen the destroyed hard drive, and probably the dismantled computer too. Past the point of no return in the madness overtaking him, the next step in obliterating the previous life was destroying the hard drive. Having cut off contact with his father and brother a couple of years before, his mother was the only continuity with regard to the family unit which had been a staple for Adam Lanza. The only other staple of significance was the computer with its ability to bring video games to life and to connect with other players when this was desired. Besides the mother, the only other primary, consistent means of connection with the world outside the home and apart from himself was the computer. And Adam Lanza knew enough about computers to know this connection and the sense of participation and other satisfactions afforded him by the computer were based on its hard drive.

Neither first responders or following investigators report that Lanza destroyed any video games. One might expect that he would have considering that he was an avid, obsessive video-game player; and when and in destroying the hard drive, he was instinctively, compulsively trying to obliterate his past. The close-by video games would appear to be something else Lanza would destroy in trying to obliterate his past since they were so obviously a central, essential part of his life and his identity. However, knowledgeable about computers as he was, Lanza knew he didn't have to destroy any videos. In destroying the hard drive, he would in effect be destroying the video games in the sense of rendering them useless in that there was no workable computer for them. That Lanza did not destroy any video games is seen as the economy of his movements--the deadly economy of the predator once any guises have dropped away--as he was preparing psychically and practically for the coming massacre, i. e., as the madness that was steadily and irreversibly consuming him was preparing him. Lanza was not rushing, nor did he feel rushed or pressured. The madness had everything under control.

Destroying at least a couple or few video games might be seen as something symbolic Lanza would have done, perhaps to go along with or supplement the murder of his mother and the destruction of the hard drive, or as confirming or reinforcing these other acts of obliteration as an iteration of them or to give them depth. However, to look for symbols or to read actions as symbols is to fail to achieve any grasp of madness and to misperceive it. The more one makes symbols out of physical factors (e. g., weapons, clothing, bodily movements, locations) attendant with an instance or episode of madness, the less one comes to know about its true nature. Grasping madness so as to see into its sources even though these cannot be fully fathomed and to see the inner, eerie unity of madness making a mockery of common grounds for stability and interaction requires flexible imagination and much exposure to human nature, not interpretation of symbols. Grasp of madness is more like anthropology than literary criticism; more like trying to understand another culture, perhaps a vanished culture, than the detached consideration of symbols or other effects in a literary work.

Adam Lanza did not kill his mother to symbolically make a point or express a belief, sentiment, or purpose. He was not trying to communicate anything to anyone else, no more than one eating a meal is trying to communicate anything to anyone else. One eats a meal because this is biologically, organically, necessary for one's sustenance. Lanza killed his mother and destroyed the hard drive because this is what the madness needed for sustenance. The less that Adam Lanza had to refer to or to reach out to--to reach back for--relating to his prior psyche and identity, the stronger the madness (its grip) became.

9. Dark Transformation

The sense of emptiness of the Yogananda Street house and sense of its isolation determined the madness would have to extend beyond it for the madness to have the required material quality and to fulfill its perverse purpose. But before leaving the house for the fulfillment of the madness, there was one more simple, yet singular and irreversible action to take. This act was putting on the black military-style pullover and the black military-style cargo pants. Though this would ordinarily be no more than a change of clothing, in the perverse world Lanza was by now immersed in, this would have singular significance.

With the mother and hard drive destroyed, the next stage of the madness--completion of transformation of person--was simple and easy, nothing more than putting on a change of clothes. Different clothing from his typical wear would energize Lanza for the coming stages of the madness that had been planned. In addition to the military-style cargo pants and pullover, Lanza had on a utility vest when he assaulted the school, not the body armor or bulletproof vest he was at first reported to be wearing. The first report of body armor or bulletproof vest raised questions as to where he had gotten it. As Connecticut officials confirmed in the later clarification noting the utility vest, there are restrictions and prevention's in buying body armor or bulletproof vests in Connecticut. They question however is moot as Lanza is now confirmed to have been wearing a utility vest with multiple pockets where he carried ammunition for the guns he brought into the school for the rampage.

With the most significant and affective references to prior psyche and identity--the mother and the hard drive--destroyed, Lanza progressed to the next steps of the transformation empowering him to carry out unspeakable acts. Killing the mother and destroying the hard drive did not provide the positive source Lanza needed for the organization, exertion, focus, and demented logic of the level and extensiveness of the urge to massacre he was being driven by.

If Lanza did not accomplish the next acts, did not reach the next stages and depths of madness, he would have committed suicide after killing his mother and destroying the hard drive; or alternately he would have collapsed in some corner of the house where he eventually would have been found by police having been alerted by a neighbor, workman, or the husband or brother that something seemed wrong at the house as there had been no contact with Nancy Lanza. If Lanza's outbreak of madness did not end in the finality of suicide in the house and he were found still alive collapsed somewhere, he would be muttering incoherently and looking around vulnerably and quizzically. He would not realize that someone, probably a police officer or mental-health worker, was here to take him away, and would be wondering why he was.

If obliterating the past and the prior self as murky, mood-filled, and sometimes taunting as this was were the intent of the madness possessing Lanza, he would have committed suicide or collapsed after killing the mother and destroying the hard drive. But the madness was not spent after these first acts because obliteration of the past and the self allowing for a sense of the past as murky, mood-filled, and sometimes taunting or painful as this self was was not the purpose and goal of the madness he was being possessed by. Adam Lanza's madness could not end by suicide or exhausted collapse in the house.

That the roomy Yogananda Street house seemed so empty despite the computer, the video games, and the attentive mother caused the madness to seek apotheosis beyond the mother's murder and the destruction of the hard drive, and a suicide following these. The Yogananda Street house's distance from other houses in this neighborhood of similar large homes on plots of acres of land among large wooded areas and fields intensified the seeming emptiness of the house. Lanza felt remote both mentally and physically. His mother's trusted attendance on him and the computer games were not enough to fill the feeling of emptiness-- the void--within Lanza where madness gestated. Cruelly, as how madness is cruel, the killing of the mother was required for obliteration of the past because of her attention to Lanza he had grown to trust from so long a period of it. While Lanza would not trust the computer games in the same way, his preoccupation with them was a characteristic the madness had to destroy utterly as well to achieve full, unrivaled control. For the madness to unequivocally, awfully demonstrate its dominance and strength, Lanza had to destroy what he trusted most giving him kinds of sustenance he could not find in himself or in the outside world and thus giving him a meager and eventually violently rejected continuity to his life. In the case of Lanza's narrow life, these trusted elements were his mother and the vital hard drive of his computer. In destroying these, he was being initiated into madness.

10. A Utility Vest, Not Body Armor

Early reports on the massacre said that Adam Lanza was wearing body armor. About three weeks later in the course of the incident as a criminal investigation, this was corrected by confirming that Lanza's outer garment was not body armor, but instead a utility vest, sometimes referred to as a sportsman's or fisherman's vest. Throughout this section, I will call it a utility vest. Such a vest is familiar because as its name implies, it has many uses. It is rugged, and has many pockets down its front of different sizes used by fishermen, hunters, campers, carpenters, hikers, electricians, construction workers, and such to carry and have handy small assorted objects they might need for the recreation or work they are engaged in. The pockets of Lanza's utility vest were filling with ammunition for the guns he had with him.

Mistaking the utility vest for body armor in seeing Lanza's body after he committed suicide in teacher Victoria Soto's classroom is understandable. The reports of body armor probably came from one or two first responders who were reporting on what they had presumed in light of the high-powered rifle closely resembling a military assault rifle used in the shootings, the black military-style pullover and cargo pants Lanza was wearing, the number of children's and teachers' bodies and the obvious damage done to them making the scene look like a military raid, and the large amount of ammunition in the pockets of the vest which would look like the heavy, conspicuous padding of body armor. First responders and early investigators would not have examined Lanza's body closely, but made sure to keep it where it was and in the position it was for the crime-scene investigators including medical examiners soon to come. The ammunition would probably not have been removed from the pockets of the utility vest, especially since Lanza was dead. If any ammunition were removed, probably not all of it would have been; remaining ammunition thus still appearing as body-armor padding. Lanza's body including what he was wearing was part of the crime scene; and crime-scene investigators and medical examiners would want to see it just as it had been found by first responders. Only later after the body had been taken away probably enclosed in a body bag would investigators remove all the ammunition from the pockets and confirm Lanza had been wearing a utility vest, not body armor of any sort.

Thoughts on the utility vest Lanza was wearing compared with the body armor he was at first mistakenly thought to be wearing shed light on Lanza's frame of mind for the attack and his planning for it. The assumption of body armor made by first responders and reported throughout the media also evidence prevailing stereotypical considerations and deductions exemplifying how foreign and incomprehensible madness is in general. Assuming the fishing vest Lanza was wearing was body armor and that this was widely accepted by media and the public for so long evidences what the public and even many law-enforcement professionals and other first responders such as firemen and EMT personnel drawn from the general population assume about insanity and popular culture. For example in this case, the assumption that Lanza was wearing body armor ascribes expectations about self-preservation and related self-defense to him that do not apply. Mistaking the utility vest for body armor also reveals misconceptions about particular ways violent video games affect an unstable, disturbed individual attached to them; which misconceptions are formed not only from violent, militaristic video games themselves, but also from ads for such games and movies imitating them prevalent in the popular-culture media.

The assumption that Lanza was wearing body armor, for instance, comes from the more general assumption that along with the associated weaponry, the concentrated area of the slaughter, and the horrific body damage of the victims, Lanza was playing out fantasies spawned by the violent video games he played. However, it was while playing the video games that Lanza was playing out any fantasies that might have been spawned. The massacre was no fantasy. Solitary and with no role models, for Lanza the video games provided models for characters and their appearance and for behavior within a defined field. The video games were like an archetype giving structure to the madness. Lanza's repetitive playing of them brought him an intimacy with the madness and with this, its dominance over him. But the video games were not the source of the madness. This is different from being a cause or progenitor of madness.

The early reports that Lanza had on body armor raised two questions which received no attention in that these reports conformed to prevailing assumptions about madness, self-defense, and video games. The first of these is the simple question, "Where did Lanza get the body armor?" The official correction that Lanza was wearing a utility vest described as a "fishing-type vest" noted also that there is a law in Connecticut restricting the purchase of body armor, defined as any "material designed to provide bullet penetration resistance." This law has been in place since 1998 when state law-enforcement officials asked legislators for such a law when they started confronting criminals who were wearing body armor. One of the provisions of this law is that sales must be made in person only in certain designated places, and body armor cannot be delivered by shipping. This automatically rules out online sales or over-the-phone purchases where delivery would have to be made by shipping. It is doubtful Lanza knew of these restrictions. In any event, body armor is not something he would have tried to purchase to have shipped to the Yogananda Street house. It would be impossible for him to be sure his mother would not know about the delivery, likely by being the one to accept it. Even if Lanza did manage to have the delivery of body armor kept from his mother's knowledge, there was the question of where to keep it once it was delivered unknown to her.

Occasionally Lanza was out of the house on his own--likely to buy the utility vest, for instance--when his mother would be home; and she could find concealed body armor during one of these times. Delivery would also entail a company's record of the sale with address of the buyer and the probability of the delivery person knowing the content of the delivery and the possibility of a delivery person seeing Lanza if he, not his mother, accepted the delivery.

If Lanza did look into legally purchasing body armor in the state, he would have learned that a sale had to be made in person with respective record of the sale and inevitable seeing him--i. e., knowing who Lanza was as the buyer--by the seller. Had Lanza considered using body armor at all, he would have quickly dropped this idea in running into state requirements regarding its purchase and also realizations about premature exposure of his plot. Trying to get body armor would have involved levels of interaction with others and records of something about his mind and specific behavior of his Lanza had shunned all his life. Instinctively secretive and dissembling regarding his plot for massacre, Lanza would not have taken any chance that this would be ruined by trying to get body armor. Especially since body armor would be extraneous.

Body armor did not figure into Lanza's plan; there was no reason for it. Lanza's purchase and use of the utility vest is a point of the practicality in his plan, not of his recreating a functional self to carry it out. Besides being sturdy and having many pockets, the vest was cut off at the shoulders, allowing for easy movement in shooting a hand weapon. Body armor by comparison would be cumbersome--thus impractical for the type of assault Lanza planned and the quickness, almost deftness, with which it was carried out. Though Lanza was not said to be athletic, by careful planning particularly with respect to choice of familiar weapons, knowledge of the layout of the school, and preselection of primary targets at the school, he was able to move quickly and with deadly efficiency. Moreover, body armor was anomalous given that Lanza committed suicide almost immediately upon realizing that first responders were in the school and were closing in on him. From all the evidence leading up to the assault and its summarily ending in suicide with the approach of the first responders, Lanza knew that his existence would be ending as the last act of the series of acts he had planned. One can't ever get much at what was in the mind of an individual or mass murderer who commits suicide. Nonetheless, with the finality that is a theme running through Lanza's case as seen in its early stages of the mother's murder and destruction of the hard drive, the multiple times each young victim was shot, and other specifics, the suicide is seen as the expected, natural, and in hindsight predictable end. Given these facts, body armor makes no sense.

Lanza was not concerned about protection of himself. Relying on the element of surprise and choosing unarmed, unsuspecting victims who would not know how to react to the assault and who were physically weak besides, along with the realization--more of a sense--that the end of his existence would occur almost simultaneously with the end of the massacre however this came (e. g., running out of ammunition, approach of armed police), protection of himself was not a part of Lanza's plans nor of his state of mind for the massacre.

Assessment of the reasons for Adam Lanza's outer body wear of the utility vest for the school assault leading to the regard of it as practical not only sheds light on aspects of the mentality going into the plan for the massacre, but also by way of comparison with the body armor first believed to have been worn brings into focus the special, transformational purpose of the military-style clothing.

11. Brother's ID and Earplugs

Military-style clothing on and the guns selected to take to the school along with a large quantity of ammunition, Lanza could have left the house then in his mother's car, and nothing would have changed. Yet a few details calling for comment appear. Seemingly incidental and arbitrary, they are neither practical or psychic; and anything that can be said about them is speculative, as with the amount of change or a candy bar found in a suicide's pocket. All that can be said about them is that despite the inexorable logic of madness--as seen in Lanza's careful, thorough plan--the anomalies and trivia of any human life find a way in.

The two inexplicable details of Lanza's rampage are his brother Ryan's identification document found on Adam Lanza's body and earplugs he was reported to be wearing about three weeks into the investigation.

Before leaving the house, Lanza put an identification document of his brother Ryan's into his pocket. One assumes he did this in the basement bedroom since reports have said that the brother used the basement bedroom until he left home after finishing college and getting a job. The document was probably outdated, and Ryan had just left it behind when he moved out of the basement. One can only wonder why Adam Lanza did this. It doesn't seem it would be instinctive as trying to clutch a bit of the past even though he had done acts of destruction to obliterate it only a short time ago. There is nothing to indicate Adam Lanza had second thoughts at any point. Nor would he have taken the document with the intention of trying to put anyone on the wrong track as to who had committed the crimes. Adam Lanza wasn't trying to trick anyone, or to disguise who he was. He left his mother where he shot her. Her car was left in the open near the front entrance of the school.

The brothers weren't close. Ryan Lanza hadn't seen his brother in two or more years. They were two different types of persons. Those who knew Ryan knew he couldn't be the one who had committed the massacre when his name was first mentioned on the basis of his identification document found on the body of Adam Lanza. One assumes the document was in the basement, and putting it in a pocket of the black clothes he had on for the massacre was a simple motion. It doesn't make sense to think that Adam Lanza would have gone into a drawer to take it out or gone anywhere in the house, perhaps to a desk in a den, where he knew it was to get it to take with him. There is no good answer to why he had it. Since Adam Lanza was obviously not trying to hide anything to try to get away with the crimes, the answer which comes to mind is the document was taken for sentimental reasons. Adam Lanza took the brother's document for the same reason a normal person would carry a memento of a relative--namely, sentimental reasons. Yet given the killing mood Lanza was in wearing the black clothes, one does not see how it would be possible for any sentiment, even a sliver, to figure in. Moreover, sentiment of the degree where one would carry a memento of a close relative is not a feeling which comes and goes. Lanza must not have had any other identification on him giving his true name, or police would not have at first given the name Ryan Lanza as the gunman who had attacked the school. So there is no reason to believe that Adam Lanza carried the brother's identification along with any identification documents of his own of the sorts carried by all adults when they go out. The brother Ryan's identification was the only one he had.

Eliminating duplicity or sentimentality as explanations for the brother Ryan's identification, this identification Adam Lanza had on him can be seen as a ring (i., e., circle) giving him an extra measure of remove--i. e., distance, protection--from the situation he created. The black, military-style clothing sealed the transformation to utter madness. The clothing made Lanza so that he could and would commit madness. But the transformation, genuine and powerful as it was, could not purge every detail of Lanza's prior being. Lanza had always been uncomfortable and uneasy around others. He had never learned to make an entrance so he could smoothly take part in a group. Even with the awful, decisive, draconian power Lanza's madness gave him over others-- the power of life and death--the characteristic, congenital, uneasiness around others stirred with the attendant responses to provide distance and protection. Responses had customarily been shyness, muteness, and awkwardness. The madness did purge the shyness. There would be nothing shy about Lanza in the rampage at the school. But the madness could not purge the desire for distance and protection the shyness was an affect to bring about.

That Lanza was wearing earplugs has been reported during the first week of the new year (January 2013). One comment quoted in a news article on this raised the question of why he would have have done this by saying something along the lines that it wasn't as if Lanza was worried about damaging his hearing because he knew he wasn't going to be coming out of the school alive. One has to assume the quoted individual saying this was making a wry joke playing on the recognition of the reason individuals ordinarily wear earplugs and the fact of Lanza's suicide. That the joke--if that's what it was instead of an ignorant remark--would even come to mind however shows how many persons automatically refer to common habits and easily grasped motives to try to comprehend acts of madness. Since with acts of madness, very little is as it seems to common sense and common experience making for the working of society and language by which this is carried on, portraying madness or referring to it by comparison to common habits or motives misrepresents it so as to leave one lost with respect to any grasp of it so that the best one can do in trying to provide understanding of it is make an inane joke. Like the brother's identification document, the earplugs later reported remain outside of rational explanation even in terms of the rationale of the madman's crazed plan which does have a logic and whose actions and their sequence can be analyzed as purposeful in progressing the plan efficiently and effectively.

Someone else is quoted in the article as saying maybe Lanza wore the earplugs so he would not hear the screams of his victims. I find this too dramatic for consideration. Although Lanza's episode of madness was undeniably an acting out of something that was deeply disturbing him, there was nothing dramatic about his behavior or the objects involved in it that was dramatic. As demiurgically willful and prepared as he was, Lanza kept a distance between him and his victims. He shot his mother as she was sleeping, or still in her bed. There is no drama in shooting a helpless, probably sleeping individual. Nor is there any drama attached to the military-style clothing Lanza had on for the school assault. For example, from all reports, it was plain, strictly functional overall. There were no insignias, no headwear, no pins, nor anything else attached to the black clothing which might be used to define or classify a violent video-game figure or branch of the military Lanza was identifying with in wearing the clothing. The clothing was generic military-style clothing, giving no hint as to any figure Lanza may have been trying to identify with by wearing it to the assault. The clothing was strictly functional in minimally, though effectively completing the transformation to the persona required for Lanza to carry out the assault in the disassociative state he was in. The clothing allowed the transformation to occur efficiently; as most of Lanza's actions that day are seen as efficient.

No only his spare clothing, but Lanza's behavior at the school when the madness had reached full pitch evidenced no drama either. For example, Lanza did not taunt his victims. He made no displays that he had power over them. He did not mock their fear. From all accounts he did not interact with the victims or prospective victims, keeping the distance between himself and them. He went about the slaughtering wordlessly, as if words would insult or take from the single-mindedness of his purpose and focus. Lanza did not exclaim or shout in jubilation or glee as he was killing his victims. The only words I have seen reported that he spoke were a command to "Let me in" to one of the teachers and students barricaded in a closet. If Lanza did utter any other words, these would most likely have the efficiency and brevity of straightforward commands.

Any suggestion that Lanza was dramatically trying to realize himself or dramatically meaning to make an impression is going the wrong way in trying to understand his particular episode of madness. Although Lanza had been transformed into madness--as all ones going mad are--his basic traits, his essentials, accounting for him as an organism to put it this way, could not be entirely displaced or eliminated. The madness commandeered such essentials for its own diabolic designs. It doing this, the madness gave the traits new, fevered, psychotic colorations. The madness rendered the traits into its own instrumentalities.

Adam Lanza had never been dramatic in his life. He had never tried to project himself nor much define himself in any way. The minor, little more than incidental touch of the earplugs cannot be a sign that Lanza had been overcome by an urge to be dramatic. The implications, especially the dramatic implications, in the consideration that Lanza wore the earplugs so he would not hear the screams of his victims goes astray in following the changes he did undergo in the passage to madness. The minor touch of the earplugs can add subtleties to an analysis of the madness and Lanza as the agency of it, but cannot contradict what is indicated by the patent and thus incomparably more telling factors. For instance, the uncharacteristic clothing Lanza was wearing indicating the transformation necessary for him to commit the massacre is the primary factor for comprehending (as much as this is possible) the particular deranged state of mind.
Analysis of the spare military-style clothing Lanza had on leads to no suggestion of drama. The clothes he died in left him as anonymously present--the antipode of projection--as he had mostly been throughout his life. Anonymity does not seek drama. Lanza was not trying to make a name for himself.

Like the brother's identification paper, the earplugs were probably a seemingly incidental, trivial element which in the absence of a shyness no longer possible after the transformation brought about a substitute sensation of distance and protection. As the brother's identification paper gave Lanza anonymity, the earplugs similarly lend him a remove from the situation of the massacre. Paradoxically in keeping with the strangeness of madness, with the earplugs and brother's identification, Adam Lanza provided for the distance and protection which had long been characteristic of him so he could feel more comfortable among others as he was murdering them.

12. The Primacy of the Video Games

News accounts about the earplugs did cite one explanation for them which though admittedly speculative, was plausible for its comparison to an aspect of a common practice at firing ranges. It became known early in the investigation in connection with the several guns Nancy Lanza was quickly found to legally own that she had taken her son Adam to firing ranges. She must have done this at least several times since in the massacre, Lanza was adept at reloading clips into the Bushmaster rifle and keeping it operating. He must have handled the rifle in a stance that allowed for fire as well as facile reloading so his targets did not have time to flee (although surviving children have reported that they ran out of teacher Victoria Soto's room when there was a pause in the shooting apparently from the gun jamming or Lanza momentarily fumbling with a clip when reloading). As the common practice at firing ranges when firing at targets, Lanza probably wore earplugs when he was learning how to handle and accurately fire guns his mother owned, including the Bushmaster rifle he used, when she took him to the firing range.

Although the speculation that Lanza wore earplugs during the school massacre because this is what he would have done when shooting at the firing range is plausible, I do not think this is the reason because it gives primacy to the firing range as the affective model for the madness over the video games; whereas I think the videos games had primacy.

It's not known if Lanza wore earplugs any time when playing his video games for hours. It's doubtful that he did. A large part of the appeal of such games is the sound effects of the shooting, the shouts, the all-around violence and destruction. It has to be presumed that the hours and years playing video games were the source for the scenario Lanza planned and moved within on the day the madness broke out, not the firing range. One has to assume that the firing range was a dimension of the video-game playing, not that the video-game playing was a dimension of the firing range.

Friends of hers say Nancy Lanza introduced guns to Adam and took him to the firing range to try to develop in him a sense of responsibility. Thus one can visualize her or an instructor at the firing range alternately giving him lessons in transporting a gun, handling ammunition when loading it, care where pointing it, physical discipline required for accurate aiming, appropriate concentration, safety precautions when finishing a session of firing, awareness of the deadliness of a gun, mindfulness of the presence of others close by. It was when playing the violent video games that Adam Lanza could throw all this off and freely exercise the skills of control of a gun and marksmanship he picked up at the firing range.

Nancy Lanza may have wanted to introduce Adam to real guns in an attempt to wean him away from what she was seeing as a bad habit threatening to grow into an obsession taking her son even further from the world of others down his own dark passageway. Members of the computer club Lanza was in in his early years at Newtown High School tell how attracted he was to computer games, notably games with violence. Thus we know that as early as his early teens Lanza had been noticeably drawn to and playing violent computer games. It has been reported that Nancy Lanza took both her sons, Adam and Ryan, to the firing range at times. Ryan Lanza, now 24, had been out of the Yogananda Street house for at least four years upon finishing college and moving away to be closer to Manhattan where he took an accounting job. Thus it had been at least four years earlier when Ryan and presumably the younger Adam too had been taken by the mother to firing ranges. It was probably considerably earlier by two or more years at least when Adam had first been introduced to real guns by his mother since she would have wanted to introduce both of the boys to them at about the same time, possibly hoping Ryan's competence, attention, and sense of responsibility would make an impression on the remote, perplexing Adam.

Considering reports that Nancy Lanza had taken both the boys to a firing range and highly probable behavior of the Lanza small family unit, one presumes Adam Lanza was introduced to and received instruction regarding real guns at about the time he was demonstrably so drawn to and adept at the weaponry in violent video games. Lanza's experience with and familiarity with real guns provided him with the basis for transferring and materializing the private, dark propensities and designs kindled by the violent video games into the daily reality of others, especially his victims and those attached to them. This is why in Lanza's case of madness the material specifics--which cannot be looked at or reduced to symbols--were necessary in their irreplaceable specificity and familiar presence in Lanza's life.

Although it is natural to look at the death, pain, and savagery Lanza brought to the lives of others, the central drive of the period of madness ending with his suicide was to realize the focus, reflexes, presence, intents, and goal bound into the video games which were the only involvement where he felt alive in the communal world transpiring around him he felt closed off from. For what was for him a brief, superlative moment in a life of 20 years, Lanza asserted a presence among others with the only objects and behavior that brought out any sensations and feeling of accomplishment; which sensations and feelings were related to the video games he had become obsessed with. The episode of madness was an attempt to break away from these.

With no experience of nor recollection of success in interacting with others or participating in communal life, Lanza tried to break away in the only way he could conceive. As guns were associated with responsibility from the way his mother presented them to him, Lanza took guns and the setting of the outside world he had used them in (i. e., the firing range) as the paradigm of the communal, outside, world he longed to be a part of; which world his madness came to demand he assert himself in and make a place for himself in. With neither the background nor abilities to enter this world as others routinely do, in accordance to the demands and stratagems of madness, Lanza instinctively and determinedly worked out a pattern of behavior complete with corresponding clothing and objects to recreate the scenario he associated with responsibility which was like a currency for acceptance into the communal world and activity in it. This was his plan. The scenario he created had resemblances to both the firing range and the violent video games. With his selection of weapons and clothing, the firing range and the video games fused. Nonetheless, the video games were the dominant affective model for the madness as indicated by the small animated targets and the enclosed space--young school children in a corner of a classroom with Lanza dominating the scenario while controlling a gun.

The firing range was assimilated into the dominant affective model of the video games to give them reach and relevance beyond the basement of the Yogananda Street house; as a child might take toy trucks to a sandbox or park as an exercise of mediation between the private, solitary world of play and demonstration, interaction, and other more complex, multifaceted behavior in the public world. The element of the firing range assured that the dominant model of the video games would be reliable--functional--in the world beyond the basement. In lending the gamesmanship, use of weapons, deadly intentions, and other elements of the video games reach and relevance, the aspects of the firing range assimilated into the plan allowed the games to sustain a presence as primary source and vital reference for the massacre.

13. The End of It All

There are no causes of madness. Madness is a process. It is a process affected by a myriad of factors ranging from environment, relationships, biology, and aspects of the natural world human beings are heir to. The number of these factors and their continually changing arrangements, strength, and degree of impact is virtually infinite making madness impossible to predict. There is no formula or calculus. The process of madness is like being caught in an urgent, unrelenting undertow. One going mad becomes more and more subject to all of the environment conditions (e. g., narrowing passageway, steep banks) and dynamics (e. g., fluid dynamics, volume pressure) making for the flow.

The first instant one is trapped by these forces, there is no escape. The combination of overwhelming forces becomes like a fist closing in on one. Moments of panic, fear, and invasive sense of peril soon give way to oceanic feelings of helplessness and hopelessness. There is no escape as all the world has become a part of the flow.

Although being caught in a mighty, unyielding flow of water is a relevant metaphor for madness, madness is not like drowning; although this image is sometimes applied to it. In drowning--from vignettes I have read by individuals who have come close to drowning or have been "brought back to life" after nearly dying from drowning--one reaches a point--a stage--where from loss of oxygen, physical sensation of suspension in the water, and mental changes, one experiences a sense of calm and peacefulness, sometimes described as ecstasy. Struggle ends, fear lifts. One drifts to one's death. Most accounts of survivors of drowning are like other accounts of near-death experiences. Madness is different though.

There never is in madness--in going mad--a phase of calm and peacefulness. It is all confusion, fear, alarm. The insistent tug of the flow is constantly felt. Whereas in drowning, one may thrash or thrust this way or that believing for a while one has a chance of freeing oneself, with madness one senses from the first that all the forces of nature are conspired and directed as if summoned to hold one is their grip exactly as one is held and tugged. One has become an integer in the cosmic equation unfolding. Fear comes because it is an instinct. But one going mad senses quickly that fear cannot excite reflexes that will bring one to safety, as if rescuing one. Rather the fear heightens one's consciousness of the power of the madness. This heightened consciousness renders one's fear unassociated with any utility so that fear in its purest state becomes permanent with one like a doppelganger; and in the latter stages of madness, fear becomes almost companionable and seems to offer promises of redemption and freedom. Such is the confusion in going mad. The wickedness of madness ingeniously mutates the fear, alarm, and confusion that are common human attributes to its own devices strengthening it. Fear in its purest state, alarm rendered impotent, and confusion that is endless and bottomless become a part of the dynamic by which madness grows in strength and gains shape.

Madness works its wickedness effectively in certain vulnerable individuals because they experience its entrance as new in a way that is not disorienting, but mildly exciting and enlivening. The wickedness of madness seems in its early stages ambiguous; neither alluring nor frightening, just a new presence like a shadow cast against a wall by the changed place of the sun in its familiar circuit. The wickedness of madness in insidious--so that the normal human attributes and also an individual's idiosyncrasies and debilities leaving him vulnerable and defenseless mutate so artlessly and imperceptibly--so seemingly naturally--that this seems normal. The wickedness of madness succeeds by mastery of the wiles of familiarization.

With the ambiguity, insidiousness, and familiarization essential to the process of madness, one wades into madness as one would wade into a river to enjoy its cool waters and promises of refreshment. One does not plunge into madness as a trapdoor opening under one; although madness is often seen as an outburst set off by specific provocations. Madness lapping up to one and washing over one cannot be separated from madness entreating one and eventually seizing one. The moment of seizure after which there is no way back cannot be pinpointed. Nor does the character of the seizure have consistency. It can be sudden, violent, and incapacitating; in which case an individual will likely be committed to a mental-health institution. Or it could look like a passing fit of anger or even rage. Or the seizure could be soporific and met by the one seized with nothing more than bemusement. No one knows how any individual would go mad. Changes of what have been assumed to be an individual's nature often change. So that a surly, aggressive man will be meek and pliable. A bright, articulate women will spout gibberish. An inward and removed Adam Lanza will command a classroom filled with children.

Another metaphor for madness--which does not replace or detract from the metaphor of being caught in a current--is that an individual is consumed by madness. Madness eats away at someone so that he is inwardly completely disfigured. The individual's outer figure which had been his presence in and means of contact with his surroundings becomes virtually completely dissolved. As the individual is being consumed, his resources for flight or defense such as muscle, joints, and nerves are successively lost. Madness is cannibalistic. The similarity between madness as consuming one and madness as being caught in a current is that in either representation of the process of going mad, the individual's ability to defend himself and eventually that he should defend himself and also the knowledge including instincts and intuitions of how to defend himself are destroyed.

At some point, the forces of the current of the process of madness one is immersed in reach a cliff to become a waterfall one is a part of. At this point, one is cast off the cliff to cascade in nothingness. Forced off the cliff with the same propulsion as the flow one had become a part of, one feels invested with a sense of power. One had never felt such force before. However, this is madness casting one off into wantonness and depravity.

Over time in Adam Lanza's process of madness, depression changed into despair. The ocean of depression became a dungeon of despair. The pain was felt more keenly, the solitude became onerous, the disappointment seemed like a life sentence. Even the video games became empty and remote. Adam Lanza began planning.

Lanza's last act was committing suicide. Do not mistake this for an apology, a qualm, or a regret. Looking back over the past years of his life and forward to the shapeless years to follow, Lanza knew he would never be able to repeat or surpass what he had done that day. He accomplished what he had planned to free himself from the dungeon. There was nothing left to do but kill himself.

Made in the USA
Middletown, DE
13 January 2018